LOW-CARB
SMOOTHIES

LOW-CARB SMOOTHIES

More Than 50 Fabulous Recipes the Whole Family Will Love

DANA CARPENDER

Best-selling author of
500 Low-Carb Recipes

FAIR WINDS
PRESS
GLOUCESTER, MASSACHUSETTS

Text © 2005 by Dana Carpender

First published in the USA in 2005 by
Fair Winds Press
33 Commercial Street
Gloucester, MA 01930

08 07 06 05 04   1 2 3 4 5

ISBN 1-59233-122-X

Library of Congress Cataloging-in-Publication Data available

Cover design by Mary Ann Smith
Book design by
Laura McFadden Design, Inc.

Printed and bound in Singapore

For my brother-in-law, Jay, who drinks two smoothies a day and wisely shuns sugar.

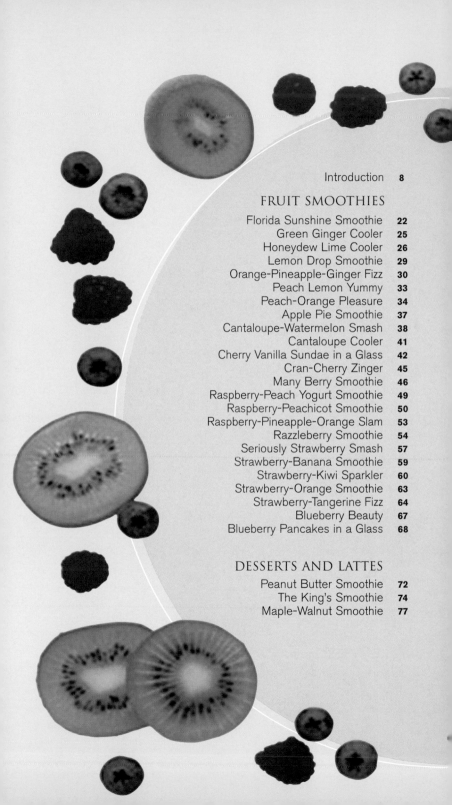

MIXED DRINK SMOOTHIES

INTRODUCTION

S moothies have taken the nation by storm! Starting as something that the health-conscious whipped up in home blenders, smoothies have emerged as one of our favorite snacks or light meals. There are prepared, bottled smoothies in every dairy case. I've even seen a smoothies kiosk at an airport!

But why buy bottled smoothies when smoothies are simplicity itself to make? You just throw your ingredients in a blender, run it until everything is—well, smooth—pour the resulting concoction in a glass, and drink it!

However, while smoothies have long been a favorite of health-conscious folks, they have usually been high carb. Many smoothie recipes call not only for fruit, but also for fruit juice, honey, ice cream, and other sugary ingredients. If you're carb-intolerant, this sort of smoothie is not your friend, no matter how many vitamins it has. I've seen plenty of smoothie recipes with as many as 60 grams of carbohydrate—that's my absolute upper limit for a day!

But with a quick rethinking of your ingredient list, low-carb smoothies are just as easy to make as the high-carb kind, and they're just as tasty, too. How easy is it to make a yummy low-carb smoothie? So easy that this is the only cookbook I've ever written where every single idea I tried was good enough to go in the book! I could have kept creating great low-carb smoothies indefinitely. So please, use this book as a jumping-off place. Try some of the recipes that sound best to you, then invent your own. I think you'll find the same thing I did—that it's nearly impossible to make a bad smoothie!

Along with keeping the carbohydrate counts low, you'll see that many of these smoothies are quite low-calorie as well—perfect for those of us who need to keep an eye on both.

INGREDIENTS

Back to that ingredient list—how will the ingredients for your low-carb smoothies differ from those for regular smoothies? First we ditch the juice altogether, except for a touch of lemon or lime juice here and there. Juice has a reputation for being healthy that it simply doesn't deserve. It's a terrific way to consume the sugar in five or six pieces of fruit, without any of the fiber that would buffer the impact on your blood sugar and make you feel full. In this book, we also lose the sugar, honey, sugar-sweetened yogurt, and regular ice cream. And we get rid of the really high-carb fruits—bananas, in particular—which are popular in smoothies, but run about 26 grams of carbohydrate apiece.

So what do we use in our low-carb smoothies?

• **Carb Countdown**—Carb Countdown dairy beverage is simply carbohydrate-reduced milk. Made by Hood Dairies, Carb Countdown is nationally distributed, and it comes in full-fat, low-fat, non-fat, and a truly fabulous chocolate-flavored. Not only does Carb Countdown have less carbohydrate than milk, it has more protein and calcium, too. Look for Carb Countdown in the dairy case at your grocery store.

The calorie counts in this book assume you use regular Carb Countdown, but you can use the non-fat or low-fat if you prefer. The carb counts of the recipes will remain the same, but the fat contents and calorie counts will drop. There is another brand of reduced-carb dairy beverage called Keto Milk. I haven't tried it, but I've tried other products by the same company and thought well of them. Keto Milk comes both in a powdered mix and a ready-to-drink form. Keto Milk has the advantage of not needing refrigeration (the ready-to-drink variety should be refrigerated after opening), so you can order it from the low-carb e-tailers. Keto also makes a hot cocoa mix; I'm betting you could use the prepared cocoa in place of the chocolate-flavored Carb Countdown.

If you can't get either of these, you can substitute half-and-half for the plain Carb Countdown or Keto Milk. For chocolate-flavored Carb Countdown, you can substitute half-and-half plus unsweetened baking cocoa and Splenda. Start with 1 tablespoon of unsweetened baking cocoa and a few teaspoons of Splenda per 1 cup of half-and-half and add more cocoa and Splenda to taste.

If you're on the South Beach diet or a similar program, non-fat milk is permitted; you may certainly use it in place of Carb Countdown in any of these recipes. Remember that milk has 12 grams of carbohydrate per cup (though lactose is a pretty benign carb, as carbs go) and adjust your daily carb count accordingly. You may also want to add a little protein powder to make up for the fact that milk has less protein than Carb Countdown, but that's up to you.

• **Cocoa powder**—This is not hot chocolate mix! We're talking unsweetened baking cocoa here, which is great for intensifying chocolate-flavored smoothies. Cocoa powder is available in the baking aisle of any grocery store.

• **Coconut milk**—This is available in cans in the Asian section of big grocery stores or in Asian markets. Locally I can buy both regular and light coconut milk. These have the same carb counts, so I used light coconut milk for the lower calorie count. However, feel free to use full-fat coconut milk if you prefer.

• **Diet soda**—Diet soda adds an appealing zing and fun flavors to smoothies. I've used Diet Rite kiwi strawberry, red raspberry, tangerine, and white grape flavors, along with sugar-free ginger ale. They're available everywhere, of course!

• **Flavorings and extracts**—You're sure to have vanilla extract on hand, but I've also used almond, coconut, orange, peppermint, rum, and walnut extracts. You'll find them in the baking aisle at your local grocery.

• **Flaxseed meal**—This is optional. You can leave it out of the recipes that call for it if you like, and you certainly can add it to any smoothie you like. There are several good reasons to add flaxseed meal to your smoothies. It's full of soluble fiber, which will thicken up your smoothies. That's not all, though. Flaxseed

meal is a good source of omega-3 fatty acids, similar to those in fish, so it's good for your heart, your skin, and even for reducing inflammation. It makes your smoothies more filling, too.

I buy Bob's Red Mill brand flaxseed meal, but you can buy whole flaxseeds at health food stores and grind them in an electric coffee grinder. (You might want to keep a grinder just for this purpose, unless you're making coffee-flavored smoothies.) Either way, store your flaxseed meal in your freezer because its fats are quite perishable.

Why not just put whole flaxseeds in your smoothies, and let the blender grind them up? I used to do this, but I'd always have big enough pieces of flaxseed that they were noticeable. With the flaxseed meal, I don't notice any grittiness or bits of seeds at all, and my flax doesn't settle to the bottom of my glass.

• Guar or xanthan—These two substances with the odd names are familiar to anyone who has been cooking low carb for a while. All they are is very finely powdered, highly refined soluble fibers. They have no flavor of their own; they just add body and creaminess to our smoothies, which is exactly what they also do in many popular processed junk foods. Find guar or xanthan—either one is fine—at health food stores or order them online.

You can simply spoon either one of these thickeners into your blender. If you do so, start with ¼ teaspoon and work your way up carefully; these thickeners are powerful! If you add too much, you'll be spooning your smoothie out of the blender.

Another great way to use guar or xanthan—the way I usually handle them—is to keep whichever thickener you've got in a salt shaker or old spice jar with a shaker top and sprinkle it into your smoothie as the blender is running. Again, watch your quantity! It's easy to add guar or xanthan, but it's impossible to remove it. I've also tried a blend of guar and xanthan called Quick Thick'ner. It's made by Gram's Gourmet, and it comes conveniently packaged in a shaker. This is good stuff, and boy, does it thicken!

I've listed guar or xanthan in those smoothies where I used it, but feel free to use it in any smoothie you think could be a little thicker. It won't change the flavor at all. And you can leave out the guar or xanthan if you prefer your smoothies thinner or if you just don't have any on hand.

As I mentioned earlier, flaxseed is another thickener you could add to smoothies. I generally use either flaxseed meal or guar or xanthan, not both.

• **Ice**—Feel free to add 1 or 2 ice cubes to any smoothie that you feel needs to be frostier, though you probably won't need it in the ones that use frozen fruit or ice cream. It's a good idea to add ice cubes one at a time and wait till one's pretty much ground up before adding another.

• **Instant coffee crystals**—You'll need these for making latte smoothies, of course! Any brand of freeze-dried instant coffee crystals should do fine. I like to keep both regular and decaf on hand so I can get the degree of "zoom" I want.

• **Lemon and lime juice and zest**—I confess, if I'm not using the zest of the lemon or lime, but only the juice, I sometimes cheat and use bottled. By the way, if you don't yet have a microplane grater, you'll be more inclined to grate fresh citrus zest if you acquire one!

• **Light mango juice**—Minute Maid puts out a light juice in Mango Tropical flavor. I've used it in just one or two smoothies in this book to get a tropical flavor. If you're a fan of those cocktails with the little umbrella on top, look for this ingredient at your grocery store.

• **Low-carb ice cream**—There are a number of low-carb, no-sugar-added ice creams available now.

Any of them should work fine in these recipes, though your final carb count will vary a bit depending on which you use. In developing these recipes, I used Atkins Endulge and Edy's Carb Benefit, but Breyer's also makes a good low-carb ice cream called CarbSmart.

• **Low-sugar fruits**—There's a common myth that a low-carb diet can't include fruit, but there are low-sugar fruits and high-sugar fruits. Apricots, berries, kiwifruits, melons, peaches, and sour cherries have been used in various recipes in this book, and while those recipes tend to be higher carb than the recipes that use only carb-free flavorings, they are also more nutritious, and the carb counts are low enough for most folks who aren't on Atkins Induction or very restricted diets.

Fruit for smoothies is best frozen before use. You use the fruit frozen, too; don't thaw it first. For this reason, I simply buy unsweetened frozen peach slices, mixed berries, raspberries, and strawberries. I bought tubs of precut melon chunks at the grocery store and stashed them in the freezer, then eyeballed my quantities. If you actually measure ½ cup of cantaloupe or honeydew chunks once or twice, you should be able to approximate easily.

For the couple of recipes using apricots, I bought them fresh, split them and removed the stones, sealed them in a plastic bag, and froze them in the freezer overnight.

Several of the recipes call for sour cherries. These are available canned in water in many grocery stores; don't buy sugar-laden "cherry pie filling" instead! I confess I didn't bother to freeze these before use. I found that the leftover cherries kept fine for at least a week in the fridge.

Cranberries, which I've used in a few recipes, are only available in the autumn. However, they freeze beautifully. So if you're a cranberry fan, pick up a few bags of cranberries when they're in season, throw them in the freezer, and you'll have cranberries for smoothies all year.

• Natural peanut butter—This is the stuff with the layer of oil on top; it's made from ground peanuts and salt, and nothing else. (You can even get it without the salt, if you prefer.) Most big grocery stores carry this with the "regular" peanut butter; if you can't find natural peanut butter in your local market, any health food store will have it. Stir it up when you get it home and store it in the fridge, and it won't separate again.

Why natural peanut butter instead of Skippy, Jif, or the like? Because "regular" peanut butter has added sugar. It also has hydrogenated oil, similar to vegetable shortening, which is why it doesn't separate and why it has that sort of plasticky consistency. If there's anything in the world worse for you than sugar, it's hydrogenated oil. Steer clear.

There is now low-carb peanut butter on the market. It doesn't have the sugar, but it does have the hydrogenated oil, and it also has soy added. For reasons explained on page 18, I minimize my soy intake. So why buy extra-expensive specialty foods, when the best choice is clear?

• Protein powder—Protein powder adds body to smoothies, and of course it also adds vital, appetite-sating, muscle-building protein. To keep it simple, I have used only vanilla- and chocolate-flavored whey protein powders in these recipes. I prefer whey protein because it is of excellent nutritional quality, dissolves without grittiness, and tastes good, too. I use Designer Whey brand, available at GNC stores in malls everywhere, but any whey protein that has no sugar should do fine.

Feel free to add protein powder to those recipes that don't call for it if you want a more filling smoothie. You'll change the flavor a tad, but vanilla-flavored protein powder seems to blend well with most flavors.

• Splenda—The carb counts in this book assume that where Splenda is listed, you'll use granular Splenda, the stuff that comes in bulk in a box or baker's bag. You can use the packets instead if you like. One packet of Splenda has the same sweetness as 2 teaspoons of granular Splenda. If you use packets, your smoothie will come out just a tad lower carb, too, because the stuff in the packets isn't bulked as much as the granular.

• Sugar-free drink mixes: Crystal Light drink mixes come in a wide variety of fruit flavors and are available in grocery stores coast-to-coast, so I used them quite a lot in these recipes. Feel free to use house brands instead; they work fine. I have also tried using Wyler's sugar-free drink mixes, and they work nicely, too.

Please note that sugar-free drink mixes are always used in powder form in these recipes, not stirred into water.

• Sugar-free pancake syrup—Just a couple of recipes in this book use sugar-free pancake syrup to give a maple flavor. Available in most grocery stores, it is made from sugar alcohols, aka polyols, and is pretty much indistinguishable from sugary pancake syrup.

• Sugar-free syrups—You know those syrups you see in fancy coffee joints? They come in sugar-free formulations and offer a tremendous range of flavors to our smoothies! The all-time champ for variety in sugar-free syrups is DaVinci, whose Splenda-sweetened syrups come in a boggling array—49 flavors, last I counted! Atkins makes a few, including caramel, chocolate, hazelnut, raspberry, strawberry, and vanilla. Either brand will work fine, as should any other brand of this sort of thing.

You can probably find some of these syrups at coffee shops, but there are a lot of flavors used here—like banana, green apple, and pineapple—that aren't likely to be used in coffee and therefore aren't likely to be sold in coffee shops. Shopping online is your best bet. I ordered my syrups directly from DaVinci, but a quick Web search should turn up dozens of e-tailers happy to ship you syrups.

The DaVinci syrups come in big bottles—750 ml, the size of a standard wine bottle—so it's good to know that they keep indefinitely. I love mine, and having acquired them for this project I'm finding many uses for them. I'm beginning to wonder how I lived without them!

Be aware: "Chocolate sugar-free syrup" in the recipes in this book refers to the coffee flavoring–type syrup, not to sugar-free Hershey's-type chocolate syrup, though such a thing does exist.

• **Yogurt**—I'm out to spread the word that plain yogurt is okay for low-carbohydrate diets! The nutrition label will read 12 grams of carbohydrate per cup, but as Jack Goldberg and Karen O'Mara pointed out in their terrific book *GO-Diet*, that's inaccurate. It's true that milk has 12 grams of carbohydrate per cup, in the form of lactose. But when milk is made into yogurt, most of the lactose is converted into lactic acid, giving yogurt its characteristically tangy flavor and leaving only 4 grams of usable carbohydrate behind.

Reading this, I added yogurt back to my low-carb diet, and I've had no trouble at all. I'm convinced that Goldberg and O'Mara are right. So I have used plain yogurt extensively in these recipes, and the carb counts given reflect Goldberg and O'Mara's revised carb count of 4 grams.

The recipes in this book call for plain non-fat yogurt, and the calorie counts reflect that, but you can use low-fat or full-fat yogurt if you prefer. The carb counts will not change.

It's very important to note that the vast majority of flavored yogurts are far higher in carbohydrate, from fruit, thickeners, and especially from sugar. So stick to plain—it's very easy to flavor it yourself.

Soy Milk and Protein Powder

To forestall the inevitable question: If you want to use soy milk or soy protein powder in these recipes, I can't stop you. However, I will give you these two warnings:

One, most soy milk has substantial amounts of sugar added to it, in one form or another—often as malt syrup. It's at least as high carb as regular milk, and often higher carb. Because lactose (milk sugar) has a low glycemic index, the carbohydrate in soy milk has a higher blood sugar impact than that of regular milk. There is unsweetened soy milk out there, but it tends to have an unpleasantly beany flavor.

Two, despite soy's reputation as the Ultimate Health Food of All Existence, there is plenty of reason to limit your soy intake. Soy has been known for several decades to interfere with thyroid function, and a slow thyroid is the last thing you need if you're trying to lose weight. More alarming, a study done in 2000 in Hawaii turned up a strong correlation between tofu consumption in middle age and cognitive impairment in old age. Researchers suspect that the problem is caused by those soy estrogens we've been told are so great for us. If that's the case, then all unfermented soy products, including soy milk and soy protein powder, will have the same effect. I really can't recommend using soy milk, or soy protein powder either.

THE NUTRITION COUNTS IN THIS BOOK

You'll find a range of carb counts in the recipes in this book, from as low as 4 grams of usable carb, through a high of 17 grams of usable carb. It's up to you to pick and choose among these recipes with an eye to the carb counts, as well as to what flavor combinations appeal to you.

You'll find a range of protein counts, as well. Some of the yogurt smoothies, where I didn't want a vanilla flavor mellowing the tang of the fruit, have as little as 13 grams of protein—about what you'd get from two eggs—while others, with added protein powder, run as high as 49 grams.

Because all of these smoothies are fairly high in protein, I see them as substantial snacks or meal replacements, not as beverages. I'd be unlikely to drink one with other food.

Note that the nutrition information for each recipe in this book is for just one serving. Many of the recipes make generous amounts, so of course they can be shared. Just divide the nutrition information accordingly.

Do You Need a Smoothie Maker?

There are now smoothie makers on the market. These are blenders that are cone-shaped to funnel ingredients into the blades and with a spigot on the side. I know folks who have smoothie makers and like them, but I use a 1970s-model Oster blender, and it works just fine. Otherwise, I wouldn't bother taking up valuable kitchen space with a one-use appliance.

Don't try making a smoothie in your food processor, though. They're too likely to leak, and it's too hard to pour a smoothie from a food processor into a glass.

FRUIT SMOOTHIES

Here are all of your favorite fruit flavors, minus all the sugar from juice. I've kept all the real fruit I could without spiking the carb counts. After all, fruits add vitamins and minerals, and most fruit carbs are at least pretty low impact. It's up to you to decide how many grams of carbohydrate you can tolerate at a time, even of "good" carbs.

You'll see that yogurt is a common denominator here. That's because yogurt blends well with every imaginable fruit flavor, and it is low carb, full of calcium, and may even be good for your immune system. Enjoy!

FLORIDA SUNSHINE SMOOTHIE

Mixed citrus flavors really sing together to make this smoothie a dose of morning sunshine in a glass.

1 cup (245 grams) plain non-fat yogurt

½ cup (120 milliliters) Carb Countdown dairy beverage

¼ teaspoon pink grapefruit sugar-free drink mix powder

⅛ teaspoon orange sugar-free drink mix powder

⅛ teaspoon sugar-free lemonade mix

Combine all of the ingredients in your blender and blend until smooth and well combined.

YIELD
191 calories,
4 g fat, 19 g protein,
5 g carbohydrate,
0 g dietary fiber,
5 g usable
carbs

GREEN GINGER COOLER

Melon balls with lime and ginger are a classic light dessert, and the same combination of flavors makes a wonderfully cooling smoothie.

1 cup (245 grams) plain non-fat yogurt

½ cup (120 milliliters) diet ginger ale

½ cup (90 grams) honeydew melon chunks or balls, frozen

¼ teaspoon lemon-lime sugar-free drink mix powder

Guar or xanthan

Combine all of the ingredients in your blender and blend until smooth and well combined.

YIELD
156 calories, trace fat,
13 g protein,
12 g carbohydrate,
1 g dietary fiber,
11 g usable
carbs

HONEYDEW LIME COOLER

This is similar to the Green Ginger Cooler, but it has a mellower flavor.

1 cup (245 grams) plain non-fat yogurt

½ cup (120 milliliters) Carb Countdown dairy beverage

½ cup (90 grams) honeydew melon chunks or balls, frozen

¼ teaspoon lemon-lime sugar-free drink mix powder

Guar or xanthan

Combine all of the ingredients in your blender and blend until smooth and well combined.

YIELD
226 calories,
4 g fat, 19 g protein,
15 g carbohydrate,
1 g dietary fiber,
14 g usable
carbs

LEMON DROP SMOOTHIE

I love lemon yogurt, and this is the drinkable version.

1 cup (245 grams) plain non-fat yogurt

½ cup (120 milliliters) Carb Countdown dairy beverage

2 tablespoons (16 grams) vanilla-flavored whey protein powder

½ teaspoon sugar-free lemonade mix

Guar or xanthan

Combine all of the ingredients in your blender and blend until smooth and well combined.

Note: For a "twist" on this smoothie, try adding ¼ teaspoon orange sugar-free drink mix.

YIELD
302 calories, 6 g fat, 40 g protein, 8 g carbohydrate, 1 g dietary fiber, 7 g usable carbs

ORANGE-PINEAPPLE-GINGER FIZZ

This smoothie has a bright and zingy flavor.

1 cup (245 grams) plain non-fat yogurt

½ cup (120 milliliters) diet ginger ale

½ teaspoon orange-pineapple sugar-free drink mix powder

1 teaspoon grated ginger root

Combine all of the ingredients in your blender and blend until smooth and well combined.

YIELD
128 calories,
trace fat, 13 g protein,
4 g carbohydrate,
trace dietary fiber,
4 g usable carbs

PEACH
LEMON YUMMY

The lemon really punches up the flavor of the peaches.

1 cup (245 grams) plain non-fat yogurt

½ cup (120 milliliters) Carb Countdown dairy beverage

¼ teaspoon sugar-free lemonade mix

⅓ cup (85 grams) sliced peaches, frozen

1 teaspoon Splenda

Combine all of the ingredients in your blender and blend until smooth and well combined.

YIELD
215 calories, 4 g fat,
19 g protein,
12 g carbohydrate,
1 g dietary fiber,
11 g usable
carbs

PEACH-ORANGE PLEASURE

1 cup (245 grams) plain non-fat yogurt

½ cup (120 milliliters) Carb Countdown dairy beverage

½ cup (125 grams) sliced peaches, frozen

½ teaspoon orange sugar-free drink mix powder

½ teaspoon guar or xanthan

Combine all of the ingredients in your blender and blend until smooth and well combined.

YIELD
227 calories,
4 g fat, 20 g protein,
15 g carbohydrate,
2 g dietary fiber,
13 g usable
carbs

APPLE PIE SMOOTHIE

This smoothie is cinnamon-apple spicy, and the vanilla-flavored protein powder adds that à la mode note!

1 cup (245 grams) plain non-fat yogurt

½ cup (120 milliliters) Carb Countdown dairy beverage

2 tablespoons (16 grams) vanilla-flavored whey protein powder

2 tablespoons (28 milliliters) green apple sugar-free syrup

¼ teaspoon ground cinnamon

1 pinch ground cloves

Combine all of the ingredients in your blender and blend until smooth and well combined.

YIELD
303 calories, 6 g fat,
41 g protein,
8 g carbohydrate,
1 g dietary fiber,
7 g usable
carbs

CANTALOUPE-WATERMELON SMASH

If you'd like to make this even more mixed-melon-y, use half cantaloupe and half honeydew, but the color won't be as pretty.

1 cup (245 grams) plain non-fat yogurt

½ cup (120 milliliters) Carb Countdown dairy beverage

½ cup (90 grams) cantaloupe chunks or balls, frozen

2 tablespoons (28 milliliters) watermelon sugar-free syrup

Guar or xanthan

Combine all of the ingredients in your blender and blend until smooth and well combined.

YIELD
218 calories, 5 g fat,
20 g protein,
12 g carbohydrate,
1 g dietary fiber,
11 g usable
carbs

CANTALOUPE COOLER

This is one of the highest-carb smoothies in the book, but my husband loved it, and cantaloupe is extremely nutritious, so I figured I'd include it anyway.

1 cup (245 grams) plain non-fat yogurt

1 cup (180 grams) cantaloupe chunks or balls, frozen

1 teaspoon lime juice

2 tablespoons (3 grams) Splenda

Combine all of the ingredients in your blender and blend until smooth and well combined.

YIELD
184 calories, 1 g fat,
14 g protein,
18 g carbohydrate,
1 g dietary fiber,
17 g usable
carbs

CHERRY VANILLA SUNDAE IN A GLASS

Love cherry-vanilla ice cream?
Try this smoothie!

½ cup (70 grams) no-sugar-added vanilla ice cream

1½ cups (355 milliliters) Carb Countdown
dairy beverage

¼ cup (30 grams) canned sour cherries
in water, drained

2 tablespoons (16 grams) vanilla-flavored
whey protein powder

1 tablespoon (14 milliliters) cherry sugar-free syrup

½ teaspoon vanilla extract

Guar or xanthan

Combine all of the ingredients in your blender and
blend until smooth and well combined.

YIELD
335 calories,
14 g fat, 40 g protein,
13 g carbohydrate,
1 g dietary fiber,
12 g usable
carbs

42

*The carb count does not
include the polyols in the
sugar-free ice cream.

CRAN-CHERRY ZINGER

1 cup (245 grams) plain non-fat yogurt

½ cup (120 milliliters) Carb Countdown dairy beverage

¼ cup (30 grams) cranberries, frozen

¼ cup (30 grams) canned sour cherries in water, drained

2 tablespoons (28 milliliters) cherry sugar-free syrup

Combine all of the ingredients in your blender and blend until smooth and well combined.

YIELD
226 calories,
4 g fat, 19 g protein,
14 g carbohydrate,
1 g dietary fiber,
13 g usable
carbs

45

MANY BERRY SMOOTHIE

Berries are absolutely loaded with antioxidants, and they even have phyto-chemicals that help prevent blindness and cancer! Look for frozen berry blends in the freezer case at your grocery store; most carry them.

1 cup (245 grams) plain non-fat yogurt

½ cup (120 milliliters) Carb Countdown dairy beverage

½ cup (90 grams) berry blend, frozen (blueberries, raspberries, blackberries, and strawberries)

1 tablespoon (14 milliliters) strawberry sugar-free syrup

1 tablespoon (14 milliliters) raspberry sugar-free syrup

1 tablespoon (14 milliliters) blueberry sugar-free syrup

Combine all of the ingredients in your blender and blend until smooth and well combined.

YIELD
245 calories,
4 g fat, 20 g protein,
18 g carbohydrate,
3 g dietary fiber,
15 g usable
carbs

RASPBERRY-PEACH YOGURT SMOOTHIE

Once I had the raspberry-peach drink mix, adding the fruit was inevitable.

1 cup (245 grams) plain non-fat yogurt

½ cup (120 milliliters) Carb Countdown dairy beverage

¼ cup (60 grams) sliced peaches, frozen

¼ cup (60 grams) raspberries, frozen

½ teaspoon raspberry-peach sugar-free drink mix powder

Combine all of the ingredients in your blender and blend until smooth and well combined.

YIELD
224 calories, 5 g fat,
19 g protein,
14 g carbohydrate,
3 g dietary fiber,
11 g usable
carbs

RASPBERRY-PEACHICOT SMOOTHIE

Apricots are remarkably low carb, and it's a breeze to halve 'em, remove the stones, and throw 'em in the freezer overnight. Don't bother peeling your apricot before you throw it in the blender; you'll never notice the pulverized skin.

1 cup (245 grams) plain non-fat yogurt

1 cup (235 milliliters) Carb Countdown dairy beverage

1 apricot, frozen

¼ peach, frozen (about 3 slices)

¼ teaspoon raspberry sugar-free drink mix powder

Combine all of the ingredients in your blender and blend until smooth and well combined.

YIELD
282 calories,
8 g fat, 25 g protein,
14 g carbohydrate,
1 g dietary fiber,
13 g usable
carbs

RASPBERRY-PINEAPPLE-ORANGE SLAM

Wow! This is a whole lot of flavor, and the soda adds a kick.

1 cup (245 grams) plain non-fat yogurt

½ cup (120 milliliters) red raspberry Diet Rite soda

½ cup (60 grams) raspberries, frozen

½ teaspoon orange-pineapple sugar-free drink mix powder

Combine all of the ingredients in your blender and blend until smooth and well combined.

YIELD
158 calories, 1 g fat,
14 g protein,
11 g carbohydrate,
4 g dietary fiber,
7 g usable
carbs

RAZZLEBERRY SMOOTHIE

1 cup (245 grams) plain non-fat yogurt

½ cup (120 milliliters) Carb Countdown dairy beverage

⅓ cup (85 grams) raspberries, frozen

2 tablespoons (28 milliliters) strawberry sugar-free syrup

Combine all of the ingredients in your blender and blend until smooth and well combined.

YIELD
211 calories,
5 g fat, 19 g protein,
10 g carbohydrate,
3 g dietary fiber,
7 g usable
carbs

SERIOUSLY STRAWBERRY SMASH

Miss strawberry milk shakes? Not anymore!

1 cup (245 grams) plain non-fat yogurt

½ cup (120 milliliters) Carb Countdown dairy beverage

5 medium strawberries, frozen

1 tablespoon (8 grams) vanilla-flavored whey protein powder

2 tablespoons (28 milliliters) strawberry sugar-free syrup

Combine all of the ingredients in your blender and blend until smooth and well combined.

YIELD
264 calories, 5 g fat, 30 g protein, 11 g carbohydrate, 2 g dietary fiber, 9 g usable carbs

STRAWBERRY-BANANA SMOOTHIE

This is even more banana-y than the previous smoothie, so if you're a banana fan, it's for you.

1 cup (245 grams) plain non-fat yogurt

½ cup (120 milliliters) Carb Countdown dairy beverage

5 medium strawberries, frozen

1 tablespoon (14 milliliters) strawberry sugar-free syrup

2 tablespoons (28 milliliters) banana sugar-free syrup

Combine all of the ingredients in your blender and blend until smooth and well combined.

Note: For a twist on this smoothie, replace the strawberry and banana syrups with ½ teaspoon strawberry-orange-banana sugar-free drink mix powder.

YIELD
209 calories,
5 g fat, 19 g protein,
10 g carbohydrate,
1 g dietary fiber,
9 g usable
carbs

STRAWBERRY-KIWI SPARKLER

You got your kiwi strawberry soda, you got your strawberries, you got your kiwi. What could be easier? Fortunately, the combination of colors doesn't turn this smoothie brown. I was a little worried about that.

1 cup (245 grams) plain non-fat yogurt

½ cup kiwi strawberry Diet Rite soda

½ kiwi fruit, peeled
(I didn't bother to freeze mine)

5 medium strawberries, frozen

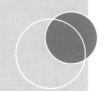

Combine all of the ingredients in your blender and blend until smooth and well combined.

YIELD
168 calories, 1 g fat,
14 g protein,
14 g carbohydrate,
3 g dietary fiber,
11 g usable
carbs

STRAWBERRY-ORANGE SMOOTHIE

1 cup (245 grams) plain non-fat yogurt

½ cup (120 milliliters) Carb Countdown
dairy beverage

4 medium strawberries, frozen

1 tablespoon (8 grams) vanilla-flavored
whey protein powder

¼ teaspoon orange sugar-free drink mix powder

Combine all of the ingredients in your blender and
blend until smooth and well combined.

YIELD
261 calories, 5 g fat,
30 g protein,
10 g carbohydrate,
1 g dietary fiber,
9 g usable
carbs

STRAWBERRY-TANGERINE FIZZ

Once again, this smoothie was inspired by the combination of flavors already in the drink mix. The Diet Rite tangerine soda really takes it up a notch, but if you can't find Diet Rite, use any diet orange soda instead.

1 cup (245 grams) plain non-fat yogurt

½ cup (120 milliliters) tangerine Diet Rite soda

5 medium strawberries, frozen

¼ teaspoon tangerine-strawberry sugar-free drink mix powder

Guar or xanthan

Combine all of the ingredients in your blender and blend until smooth and well combined.

YIELD
145 calories, 1 g fat, 13 g protein, 8 g carbohydrate, 1 g dietary fiber, 7 g usable carbs

BLUEBERRY BEAUTY

Wow, what a color! The lemon juice really brings out the flavor of the berries here.

1 cup (245 grams) plain non-fat yogurt

½ cup (120 milliliters) Carb Countdown dairy beverage

½ cup (75 grams) blueberries, frozen

3 tablespoons (4.5 grams) Splenda

1 teaspoon lemon juice

Combine all of the ingredients in your blender and blend until smooth and well combined.

YIELD
232 calories, 5 g fat,
19 g protein,
15 g carbohydrate,
2 g dietary fiber,
13 g usable
carbs

BLUEBERRY PANCAKES IN A GLASS

I figured if blueberries are good in pancakes, with syrup and all, why not try the same flavors in a smoothie?

1 cup (245 grams) plain non-fat yogurt

½ cup (120 milliliters) Carb Countdown dairy beverage

½ cup (75 grams) blueberries, frozen

2 tablespoons (28 milliliters) sugar-free pancake syrup

¼ teaspoon ground cinnamon

Combine all of the ingredients in your blender and blend until smooth and well combined.

YIELD
233 calories,
5 g fat, 19 g protein,
16 g carbohydrate,
2 g dietary fiber,
14 g usable
carbs*

*The carb count does not include the polyols in the sugar-free pancake syrup.

DESSERTS AND LATTES

Here is a series of smoothies based on well-loved candies, sundaes, cakes, and lattes. A latte smoothie is particularly great if you're in a big hurry in the morning, since it serves as breakfast and coffee all in one. But no matter what the time of day, the best thing about these recipes is that they can satisfy your junk food craving without blowing your low-carb program—you can feel virtuous while your mouth is saying "decadent"!

One small note: Please use only natural, creamy peanut butter when a recipe calls for it—the other kinds (including the new low-carb versions) are full of hydrogenated oils which are horrible for you. Trust me, your body will thank you.

PEANUT BUTTER SMOOTHIE

Remember Peanut Butter Crunch? This is Peanut Butter Smooth!

1½ cups (355 milliliters) Carb Countdown dairy beverage

3 tablespoons (50 grams) natural peanut butter

2 tablespoons (16 grams) vanilla-flavored whey protein powder

2 tablespoons (3 grams) Splenda

¼ teaspoon blackstrap molasses

Combine all of the ingredients in your blender and blend until smooth and well combined.

Note: To create a Peanut Butter and Jelly Smoothie, add 1½ tablespoons (21 milliliters) grape, raspberry, or strawberry sugar-free syrup after combining the other ingredients.

YIELD

585 calories, 36 g fat, 49 g protein, 18 g carbohydrate, 4 g dietary fiber, 14 g usable carbs

THE KING'S SMOOTHIE

Reportedly, Elvis's favorite food was fried peanut-butter-and-banana sandwiches on white bread. If he'd drunk these instead, he would have been healthier!

1½ cups (355 milliliters) Carb Countdown dairy beverage

3 tablespoons (50 grams) natural peanut butter

2 tablespoons (16 grams) vanilla-flavored whey protein powder

2 tablespoons (28 milliliters) banana sugar-free syrup

Guar or xanthan

Combine all of the ingredients in your blender and blend until smooth and well combined.

YIELD
580 calories,
36 g fat, 49 g protein,
17 g carbohydrate,
4 g dietary fiber,
13 g usable
carbs

MAPLE-WALNUT SMOOTHIE

How very New England!

½ cup (70 grams) no-sugar-added vanilla ice cream

1½ cups (355 milliliters) Carb Countdown dairy beverage

2 tablespoons (16 grams) vanilla-flavored whey protein powder

1 teaspoon walnut extract

1 tablespoon (14 milliliters) sugar-free pancake syrup

1 tablespoon (1.5 grams) Splenda

¼ cup (30 grams) walnuts

Combine all of the ingredients except the walnuts in your blender and blend until smooth and well combined. Then add the walnuts and blend just until they're chopped up a little.

YIELD
494 calories, 31 g fat, 47 g protein, 11 g carbohydrate, 2 g dietary fiber, 9 g usable carbs*

*The carb count does not include the polyols in the sugar-free pancake syrup.

VIENNESE LATTE

Show up at the office with this chocolate-
and cinnamon-laced concoction, and
you'll be the envy of all your co-workers.
Just flash 'em a grin and say, "It's my diet,
you know."

1½ cups (355 milliliters) Carb Countdown
dairy beverage

2 tablespoons (16 grams) vanilla-flavored
whey protein powder

1 tablespoon (14 milliliters) chocolate
sugar-free syrup

¼ teaspoon ground cinnamon

2 teaspoons instant coffee granules

Guar or xanthan

Combine all of the ingredients in your blender and
blend until smooth and well combined.

YIELD
313 calories, 14 g fat,
40 g protein,
9 g carbohydrate,
1 g dietary fiber,
8 g usable
carbs

HAZELNUT-AMARETTO FROZEN LATTE

This is nutty-good. Atkins makes hazelnut syrup, and DaVinci makes amaretto syrup.

½ cup (70 grams) no-sugar-added vanilla ice cream

1 cup (235 milliliters) Carb Countdown dairy beverage

1 tablespoon (8 grams) vanilla-flavored whey protein powder

1½ teaspoons instant coffee granules

1 tablespoon (14 milliliters) hazelnut sugar-free syrup

1 tablespoon (14 milliliters) amaretto sugar-free syrup

Guar or xanthan

Combine all of the ingredients in your blender and blend until smooth and well combined.

YIELD
191 calories, 9 g fat,
23 g protein,
5 g carbohydrate,
trace dietary fiber,
5 g usable
carbs

IRISH CREAM COFFEE LATTE

I found a recipe for making your own Irish cream liqueur and took it from there. My Irish cream–loving husband says I got it right.

1½ cups (355 milliliters) Carb Countdown dairy beverage

2 tablespoons (16 grams) vanilla-flavored whey protein powder

2½ teaspoons instant coffee granules

¼ teaspoon almond extract

¼ teaspoon vanilla extract

2 tablespoons (28 milliliters) chocolate sugar-free syrup

1 tablespoon (1.5 grams) Splenda

Combine all of the ingredients in your blender and blend until smooth and well combined.

YIELD
319 calories, 14 g fat,
40 g protein,
9 g carbohydrate,
1 g dietary fiber,
8 g usable
carbs

MOCHA LATTE
This is just simple mocha. Good stuff!

1½ cups (355 milliliters) Carb Countdown
dairy beverage

1 teaspoon instant coffee granules

2 tablespoons (16 grams) vanilla-flavored
whey protein powder

3 tablespoons (45 milliliters) chocolate
sugar-free syrup

Guar or xanthan

2 ice cubes

Combine all of the ingredients in your blender and
blend until smooth and well combined.

YIELD
307 calories, 14 g fat,
40 g protein,
8 g carbohydrate,
1 g dietary fiber,
7 g usable
carbs

PEPPERMINT PATTIE SMOOTHIE

This smoothie is for all you fans of Peppermint Patties and chocolate chip mint ice cream, and I know your number is legion.

1½ cups (355 milliliters) chocolate-flavored Carb Countdown dairy beverage

¼ cup (32 grams) chocolate-flavored whey protein powder

2 tablespoons (10 grams) unsweetened baking cocoa

¼ teaspoon mint extract

½ teaspoon guar or xanthan

2 ice cubes

Combine all of the ingredients in your blender and blend until smooth and well combined.

YIELD
246 calories,
5 g fat, 45 g protein,
11 g carbohydrate,
5 g dietary fiber,
6 g usable
carbs

PEANUT BUTTER CUP SMOOTHIE

Is there anyone who doesn't love chocolate and peanut butter together?

1½ cups (355 milliliters) chocolate-flavored Carb Countdown dairy beverage

3 tablespoons (50 grams) natural peanut butter

2 tablespoons (16 grams) chocolate-flavored whey protein powder

2 tablespoons (10 grams) unsweetened baking cocoa

Combine all of the ingredients in your blender and blend until smooth and well combined.

YIELD
413 calories,
26 g fat, 33 g protein,
18 g carbohydrate,
7 g dietary fiber,
11 g usable carbs

SNICKERS SMOOTHIE

Wow! Chocolate, peanuts, and the dulce de leche or caramel syrup make this too good.

1½ cups (355 milliliters) chocolate-flavored Carb Countdown dairy beverage

2 tablespoons (30 grams) natural peanut butter

2 tablespoons (16 grams) chocolate-flavored whey protein powder

2 tablespoons (28 milliliters) dulce de leche or caramel sugar-free syrup

Guar or xanthan

2 tablespoons flaxseed meal

Combine all of the ingredients in your blender and blend until smooth and well combined.

YIELD
391 calories,
23 g fat, 32 g protein,
16 g carbohydrate,
8 g dietary fiber,
8 g usable
carbs

ALMOND JOY
IN A GLASS

Make this without the almond extract
if you like for a Mounds smoothie.

1½ cups (355 milliliters) chocolate-flavored
Carb Countdown dairy beverage

2 tablespoons (16 grams) chocolate-flavored
whey protein powder

2 tablespoons (10 grams) unsweetened
baking cocoa

¼ teaspoon almond extract

¼ teaspoon coconut extract

Combine all of the ingredients in your blender and
blend until smooth and well combined.

YIELD
137 calories, 3 g fat,
24 g protein,
8 g carbohydrate,
4 g dietary fiber,
4 g usable
carbs

RUM BALLS IN A GLASS

I really did look at a recipe for Rum Balls to make this, and I got all the flavors into this smoothie. Mmmm!

1½ cups (355 milliliters) chocolate-flavored Carb Countdown dairy beverage

2 tablespoons (16 grams) vanilla-flavored whey protein powder

1 tablespoon (5 grams) unsweetened baking cocoa

¼ teaspoon walnut extract

½ teaspoon rum extract

1 teaspoon guar or xanthan

1 ice cube

Combine all of the ingredients in your blender and blend until smooth and well combined.

YIELD
126 calories, 3 g fat,
23 g protein,
5 g carbohydrate,
3 g dietary fiber,
2 g usable
carbs

CHOCOLATE-ORANGE TRUFFLE SMOOTHIE

One of my very favorite treats is Pure De-lite brand sugar-free truffles, in dark chocolate–orange flavor. When I was a kid, my favorite birthday cake was devil's food with orange icing. So I made a smoothie in the same flavor, and it's one of my favorites.

1½ cups (355 milliliters) Carb Countdown dairy beverage

2 tablespoons (16 grams) chocolate-flavored whey protein powder

2 tablespoons (10 grams) unsweetened baking cocoa

¼ teaspoon orange sugar-free drink mix powder

Guar or xanthan

2 ice cubes

Combine all of the ingredients in your blender and blend until smooth and well combined.

YIELD
328 calories, 15 g fat,
41 g protein,
13 g carbohydrate,
4 g dietary fiber,
9 g usable
carbs

BANANA SPLIT SMOOTHIE

If you like something other than chocolate syrup on your banana splits, feel free to add a little of your favorite flavor of sugar-free syrup to this smoothie.

1½ cups (355 milliliters) chocolate-flavored Carb Countdown dairy beverage

2 tablespoons (16 grams) vanilla-flavored whey protein powder

1 teaspoon vanilla extract

2 tablespoons (28 milliliters) banana sugar-free syrup

Guar or xanthan

Combine all of the ingredients in your blender and blend until smooth and well combined.

YIELD
123 calories, 2 g fat,
22 g protein,
4 g carbohydrate,
1 g dietary fiber,
3 g usable
carbs

CHOCOLATE-CHERRY SMOOTHIE

This is for all of you who are devoted to chocolate-covered cherries or Bavarian chocolate-cherry desserts.

1½ cups (355 milliliters) chocolate-flavored Carb Countdown dairy beverage

⅓ cup (35 grams) canned sour cherries in water, drained

2 tablespoons (16 grams) chocolate-flavored whey protein powder

2 tablespoons (10 grams) unsweetened baking cocoa

1 tablespoon (14 milliliters) cherry sugar-free syrup

1 tablespoon (14 milliliters) chocolate sugar-free syrup

Combine all of the ingredients in your blender and blend until smooth and well combined.

YIELD
168 calories, 3 g fat, 24 g protein, 15 g carbohydrate, 5 g dietary fiber, 10 g usable carbs

SACHER TORTE SMOOTHIE

Sacher Torte is a famous cake from a fancy Austrian hotel, combining chocolate cake and icing with apricot filling. I thought that it's famous for a reason and tried it in a smoothie. Yummy!

1½ cups (355 milliliters) chocolate-flavored Carb Countdown dairy beverage

2 apricots, frozen

¼ cup (32 grams) chocolate-flavored whey protein powder

2 tablespoons (10 grams) unsweetened baking cocoa

1 tablespoon (14 milliliters) chocolate sugar-free syrup

Combine all of the ingredients in your blender and blend until smooth and well combined.

YIELD
280 calories, 5 g fat,
46 g protein,
19 g carbohydrate,
6 g dietary fiber,
13 g usable
carbs

DEATH BY CHOCOLATE

I put every chocolate ingredient
I had on hand in this. Not surprisingly,
it was great!

½ cup (70 grams) no-sugar-added chocolate
ice cream

1½ cups (355 milliliters) chocolate-flavored
Carb Countdown dairy beverage

2 tablespoons (16 grams) chocolate-flavored
whey protein powder

2 tablespoons (28 milliliters) chocolate
sugar-free syrup

2 tablespoons (10 grams) unsweetened
baking cocoa

Combine all of the ingredients in your blender and
blend until smooth and well combined.

YIELD
137 calories, 3 g fat,
24 g protein,
8 g carbohydrate,
4 g dietary fiber,
4 g usable
carbs

CHOCOLATE-COCONUT-RUM DECADENCE

Oh, man, and this is health food?!

1 cup (235 milliliters) chocolate-flavored
Carb Countdown dairy beverage

½ cup (120 milliliters) light coconut milk

2 tablespoons (16 grams) chocolate-flavored
whey protein powder

¼ teaspoon coconut extract

¼ teaspoon rum extract

2 ice cubes

¼ teaspoon guar or xanthan

Combine all of the ingredients in your blender and
blend until smooth and well combined.

YIELD
180 calories, 8 g fat,
23 g protein,
7 g carbohydrate,
1 g dietary fiber,
6 g usable
carbs

CHOCOLATE DRINKABLE YOGURT

For the most part, I don't think the flavors of yogurt and chocolate go together. But this smoothie came out quite well. If you want the health benefits of yogurt, but are a die-hard chocoholic, this one's for you.

½ cup (125 grams) plain non-fat yogurt

1 cup (235 milliliters) chocolate-flavored Carb Countdown dairy beverage

2 tablespoons (16 grams) vanilla-flavored whey protein powder

1 tablespoon (5 grams) unsweetened baking cocoa

½ tablespoon Splenda

2 to 3 ice cubes

Combine all of the ingredients in your blender and blend until smooth and well combined.

YIELD
285 calories, 7 g fat,
41 g protein,
10 g carbohydrate,
4 g dietary fiber,
6 g usable
carbs

CHOCOLATE-RASPBERRY SMOOTHIE

This is amazing. If you're a fan of chocolate-covered strawberries, use frozen strawberries instead!

1½ cups (355 milliliters) chocolate-flavored Carb Countdown dairy beverage

½ cup (120 grams) raspberries, frozen

¼ cup (32 grams) chocolate-flavored whey protein powder

1 tablespoon (5 grams) unsweetened baking cocoa

2 tablespoons (13 grams) flaxseed meal

Combine all of the ingredients in your blender and blend until smooth and well combined.

YIELD
360 calories, 11 g fat, 49 g protein, 22 g carbohydrate, 13 g dietary fiber, 9 g usable carbs

ERIC'S VANILLA-CARAMEL SMOOTHIE

I'm the resident chocoholic, while my husband divides his sweet-lust between vanilla and caramel. So I combined the two for him and made his day!

½ cup (70 grams) no-sugar-added vanilla ice cream

1 cup (235 milliliters) Carb Countdown dairy beverage

2 tablespoons (16 grams) vanilla-flavored whey protein powder

1 tablespoon (14 milliliters) dulce de leche or caramel sugar-free syrup

½ teaspoon vanilla extract

Guar or xanthan

Combine all of the ingredients in your blender and blend until smooth and well combined.

YIELD
246 calories, 10 g fat,
33 g protein,
6 g carbohydrate,
1 g dietary fiber,
5 g usable
carbs

*The carb count does not include the polyols in the sugar-free ice cream.

EVERY GOOD THING

I heard about this flavor combination and was intrigued enough to try it. It's great!

1½ cups (355 milliliters) chocolate-flavored Carb Countdown dairy beverage

2 tablespoons (16 grams) vanilla-flavored whey protein powder

½ teaspoon instant coffee granules

⅛ teaspoon orange extract

Guar or xanthan

Combine all of the ingredients in your blender and blend until smooth and well combined.

YIELD
114 calories, 2 g fat,
22 g protein,
3 g carbohydrate,
1 g dietary fiber,
2 g usable
carbs

MIXED DRINK SMOOTHIES

While developing these recipes, I found myself perusing cocktail menus with a fresh eye, looking for new flavor combinations. Many of them were perfect! Keep an eye on those cocktail menus and give your favorites a try.

PIÑA COLADA SMOOTHIE

Coconut, pineapple, and rum—all that's missing is the little umbrella!

1 cup (245 grams) plain non-fat yogurt

½ cup (120 milliliters) light coconut milk

2 tablespoons (28 milliliters) pineapple sugar-free syrup

½ teaspoon rum extract

½ teaspoon coconut extract

Combine all of the ingredients in your blender and blend until smooth and well combined.

YIELD

197 calories, 6 g fat,
15 g protein,
22 g carbohydrate,
0 g dietary fiber,
22 g usable
carbs

STRAWBERRY DAIQUIRI SMOOTHIE

This is fresh and lively!

1 cup (245 grams) plain non-fat yogurt

½ cup (120 milliliters) Carb Countdown dairy beverage

½ lime, grated rind and juice

5 medium strawberries, frozen

3 tablespoons (45 milliliters) strawberry sugar-free syrup

½ teaspoon rum extract

Combine all of the ingredients in your blender and blend until smooth and well combined.

YIELD
221 calories, 5 g fat,
19 g protein,
27 g carbohydrate,
2 g dietary fiber,
25 g usable
carbs

JUNGLE JUICE
Here's every tropical flavor in
one smoothie.

1 cup (245 grams) plain non-fat yogurt

½ cup (120 milliliters) light coconut milk

1½ tablespoons (21 milliliters) pineapple
sugar-free syrup

1½ tablespoons (21 milliliters) banana
sugar-free syrup

½ teaspoon coconut extract

Guar or xanthan

Combine all of the ingredients in your blender and
blend until smooth and well combined.

YIELD
194 calories, 6 g fat,
15 g protein,
8 g carbohydrate,
0 g dietary fiber,
8 g usable
carbs

LIQUID CRUISE

This is my smoothie version of a cocktail served on a famous cruise line. You'll have to supply the Caribbean atmosphere yourself.

1 cup (245 grams) plain non-fat yogurt

½ cup (120 milliliters) low-carb mango juice

½ peach, frozen

1 tablespoon (14 milliliters) pineapple sugar-free syrup

¼ teaspoon coconut extract

Combine all of the ingredients in your blender and blend until smooth and well combined.

YIELD
151 calories, trace fat,
13 g protein,
10 g carbohydrate,
1 g dietary fiber,
9 g usable
carbs

CITRUS-CRANBERRY SMOOTHIE

Believe it or not, I got this combination of flavors from a martini menu! What ever happened to gin and vermouth?

1 cup (245 grams) plain non-fat yogurt

½ cup (120 milliliters) Carb Countdown dairy beverage

¼ cup (30 grams) cranberries, frozen

¼ teaspoon pink grapefruit sugar-free drink mix powder

¼ teaspoon lemon-lime sugar-free drink mix powder

Combine all of the ingredients in your blender and blend until smooth and well combined.

YIELD
202 calories, 4 g fat,
19 g protein,
8 g carbohydrate,
1 g dietary fiber,
7 g usable
carbs

ALSO BY DANA CARPENDER

500 More Low-Carb Recipes
ISBN: 1-59233-089-4
$19.95/$28.95 CAN
Paperback; 560 pages
Available wherever books are sold

If you've thought about quitting your low-carb lifestyle, it's most likely because you're bored—you just want a really, truly, interesting meal for a change. Problem solved! From quick and easy recipes for family dinners to new side dishes to go with those steak and chops to festive foods to make the holidays enjoyable without blowing your program, we have it all. Recipes include:

Thai Beef Lettuce Wraps • Un-Potato and Sausage Soup
Shrimp and Artichoke "Risotto" • Crab-Stuffed Poblano Peppers
Sesame-Almond Napa Slaw • Caribbean Grilled Chicken

200 Low-Carb Slow Cooker Recipes
ISBN: 1-59233-076-2
$17.95/$24.95 CAN
Paperback; 256 pages
Available wherever books are sold

Low-Carb Miracles from Your Slow Cooker!

For the low-carb dieter, traditional slow cooker recipes can be a problem. Many of them depend on potatoes, noodles, rice, and starchy canned soups. And if you've tried to make up your own recipes, you may have found the results less than compelling—too often the food can be mushy, water-logged, and bland. Fortunately, with *200 Low-Carb Slow Cooker Recipes*, you can use your slow cooker and follow your low-carb diet, too! While you are at work, your slow cooker can be cooking up:

Tuscan Chicken • Kashmiri Lamb Kabobs • Teriyaki-Tangerine Ribs
Orange Rosemary Pork • Chipotle Brisket • Firehouse Chili Braised
Pork with Fennel • Pizza Stew • Morty's Mixed Meat Loaf

So go ahead, plug in your slow cooker, and look forward to coming home to a fabulous low-carb supper tonight!